An Unofficial
RILKE

RAINER MARIA RILKE

Poems 1912–1926

selected, translated
and with an introduction by
MICHAEL HAMBURGER

BLACK SWAN BOOKS

Published by
BLACK SWAN BOOKS Ltd.
P.O. Box 327
Redding Ridge, CT 06876
ISBN 0-933806-17-5

Copyright © Michael Hamburger 1981

The German texts of Rilke's poems from *Gedichte 1906–1926* (1953) and *Werke* (2nd impression, 1970) are included by kind permission of Insel Verlag, Frankfurt am Main

For permission to include the poem from 'From the Remains of Count C.W.' we thank The Hogarth Press

Printed in England by Skelton's Press Ltd
Wellingborough, Northamptonshire

CONTENTS

Introduction	9
Pearls roll away . . . *Perlen entrollen . . .*	31
The Spanish Trilogy *Die Spanische Trilogie*	33
The Spirit Ariel *Der Geist Ariel*	39
Ignorant I confront the heaven of my life . . . *Unwissend vor dem Himmel meines Lebens . . .*	41
Narcissus *Narziss*	43
Christ's Descent into Hell *Christi Höllenfahrt*	45
Turning-Point *Wendung*	47
Complaint *Klage*	51
'A Man Has to Die of Knowing Them' ›*Man Muß Sterben Weil Man Sie Kennt*‹	53
Abandoned bare on the heart's mountains . . . *Ausgesetzt auf den Bergen des Herzens . . .*	55
To Hölderlin *An Hölderlin*	57
Again and again, though we know the landscape of love . . . *Immer wieder, ob wir der Liebe Landschaft auch kennen*	59
The Death of Moses *Der Tod Moses*	61
Death *Der Tod*	63

Oh, misery, my mother tears me down . . . *Ach wehe, meine Mutter reißt mich ein . . .*	65
Grey love snakes . . . *Graue Liebesschlangen . . .*	65
Not that, when (suddenly) we are grown-up . . . *Nicht daß uns, da wir (plötzlich) erwachsen sind . . .*	67
To Music *An die Musik*	69
To pass the time, to kill it: curious saying! . . . *Wunderliches Wort die Zeit vertreiben! . . .*	71
Haiku *Haï-Kaï*	71
The Hand *Die Hand*	73
Antistrophes *Gegen-Strophen*	75
We, in the grappling nights . . . *Wir, in den ringenden Nächten . . .*	77
My shy moon-shadow would like to talk . . . *Mein scheuer Mondschatten spräche gern . . .*	79
. . . When will, when will, when will they let it suffice . . . *. . . Wann wird, wann wird, wann wird es genügen*	81
As long as self-thrown things you catch . . . *Solang du Selbstgeworfnes fängst . . .*	83
We're mouths, no more . . . *Wir sind nur Mund . . .*	85
Fictitious Biography *Imaginärer Lebenslauf*	87
The Magician *Der Magier*	89
Will-o'-the-Wisps *Irrlichter*	91
A furrow in my brain . . . *Eine Furche in meinem Hirn . . .*	93

Palm of the Hand *Handinneres*	95
Mausoleum *Mausoleum*	97
Night. O face against my face . . . *Nacht. Oh du in Tiefe gelöstes . . .*	99
Gravity *Schwerkraft*	101
Now it is time that gods came walking out . . . *Jetzt wär es Zeit, daß Götter träten aus . . .*	103
Rose, pure contradiction, delight . . . *Rose, oh reiner Widerspruch, Lust . . .*	105
Gong ('Sound by hearing no longer . . .') *Gong ('Klang, nichtmehr mit Gehör . . .')*	105
Idol *Idol*	107
Gong ('Not meant for ears . . .') *Gong ('Nicht mehr für Ohren . . .')*	109
Garden, tenderly darkened . . . *Von nahendem Regen . . .*	111
Arrival *Ankunft*	113
Now come, the last that I can recognize . . . *Komm du, du letzter, den ich anerkenne . . .*	115

INTRODUCTION

I

'Fame, after all, is only the quintessence of all the misunderstandings that collect around a new name', Rilke wrote in his monograph on Rodin. If Rilke's own fame bears out the truth of that observation, it is no longer because a legend of his own making was substituted for complex and uncomfortable realities. Both Rilke's work and his person have received the most searching scrutiny and analysis. Few stones have been left unturned either by his biographers or by the editors of his works and letters, including works and letters highly adverse to the various images of himself that Rilke wished to make public at successive stages of his life.

Most of the poems chosen here are of that kind. They were left either unpublished or uncollected by Rilke in his lifetime. Such a choice would need justification in most other cases, since most authors must be allowed to be the best judges of what constitutes their canon. Yet Rilke's case is a special one, for several reasons. He himself made no provision for a clear line to be drawn between his public and private work, his public and private image; and there are good grounds for assuming that he was indifferent to the rigorous impersonality upheld – even beyond their deaths – by contemporaries like Stefan George or Hofmannsthal. Many of his letters, for instance, can rightly be regarded as part of his literary work, and may well have been written with a view to posthumous publication. For the greater part of his working life they served him not only as his main line of communication with a large circle of friends and readers, but as a complement to his poetry of a kind for which other poets have adopted more public, more impersonal media like lectures or critical essays. The many poems Rilke wrote for friends in his later years, on the other hand, may have been primarily intended as presents to those friends, but they were also a means of communication not wholly distinct from either the letters or the books to which he attached them. Certainly he himself made no rigid distinction between such dedicatory verses and any others written at the same period but never collected by him for publication in books; and even the *Duino Elegies* appeared with a dedication describing them as 'part of the property' of the lady to whom they were dedicated.

That Rilke published no major collection of poems between the second volume of his *New Poems* in 1908 and the *Duino Elegies* in 1922 is another special circumstance, and an astonishing one if we consider how much uncollected verse he produced in those years, and how much of it now seems no more private, slight or occasional than a good deal of the work he did choose to collect both before and after the intermission. The relative neglect of the miscellaneous poems of this period, as against the *Duino Elegies* and the *Sonnets to Orpheus*, does point to a triumph of the legend over the reality. Rilke had his own reasons for underrating the miscellaneous poems. Many of them were the product of a drawn-out personal crisis, precipitated by his work on the prose book *The Notebooks of Malte Laurids Brigge*, deepened by political and social upheavals brought about by the First World War, and prolonged by Rilke's failure to sustain work on the *Elegies* begun at Duino in 1912. To this we must add Rilke's conviction that a book of poems ought to be a coherent, consistent whole, held together by a dominant theme or by a structural unity. The more he felt himself to be threatened by plurality, disjunction, fortuitousness – and that threat is inseparable from the crisis – the more desperately he longed for the definitive and unified statement he had hoped to make in the *Elegies*; and the more, too, he overestimated the finality and comprehensiveness of any statement a poet of his kind is capable of making. The contradictions and ambivalences of Rilke's crisis years are as evident in the *Elegies* as in the short poems

Rilke wrote between 1912 and 1922; and the *Elegies'* very claim to finality and comprehensiveness has laid them open to radical objections on theological, philosophical and ethical grounds.

Yet just as Rilke's work cuts through distinctions between public and private writings, it cuts through distinctions between aesthetic and non-aesthetic criteria. Rilke cared as little about aspirations to the autonomy of art as about notions of the impersonality of the artist. Because, from his early years onward, he would not recognize any basic dichotomy between life and art, he could not have any use for the doctrine of 'art for art's sake'. The same blithe indifference to the battles in his time between Symbolists and Naturalists, formalists and realists, that had kept him prolific up to the writing of *Malte Laurids Brigge*, taking whatever came his way from the diverse currents and energies of the age, and assimilating it to his own powerful subjectivity, left him helpless as soon as the prose work brought him up against rifts his verse had simply skated over – not least in the *New Poems*, with their unprecedented capacity to make inwardness and outwardness reciprocal, to achieve works of pure art by a mimetic not 'low' but high, as in the poems about the Spanish dancer or the roundabout or the panther. All such achievements had been due to an unquestioned faith not in art for art's sake but rather in art for life's sake and – as far as Rilke's person was concerned – in life for art's sake. That this dual faith amounted to a tautology – a circle that, if not vicious, had no validity outside Rilke's life and work – was brought home to Rilke when he struggled with the partly autobiographical material of his prose book. As early as 1908 he tried to explain the difference to Rodin, whose example of constant attention and application had meant so much to Rilke when he set to work on the *New Poems*: 'In writing poetry one is always helped and even carried along by the rhythm of external things; for the lyrical cadence is that of nature: of waters, of wind, of the night. But to get rhythm into prose one has to go down into oneself and find the anonymous, multiple rhythm of one's blood. Prose has to be built like a cathedral.'

It is characteristic of the earlier Rilke to assume that building a cathedral is a process analogous to finding 'the rhythm of one's own blood'. As for the natural rhythms of poetry, Rilke's words to Rodin link up with his earlier reading of Nietzsche's *The Birth of Tragedy* and his marginalia of 1900 in his copy of the book. One of these marginalia is a gloss on Nietzsche's passage: 'The melody gives birth to the poetic work, and again and again, always anew; that, and nothing else, is what the *stanza form* of folk song tells us: a phenomenon I had always observed with amazement, until I found this explanation at last.' In Nietzsche's passage it is the 'spirit of music' that gives birth to poetry. In Rilke's gloss it becomes a 'flowing, unapplied force that does not enter our works in order to recognize itself in phenomena, but hovers over our heads uncaring, as though we did not exist'; and this force is identified with God. 'Music (rhythm) is the untrammelled superabundance of God, who has not exhausted himself in phenomena, and artists take up this challenge in a vague urge to complete the world in the same spirit in which this power, continuing to create, would have acted, and to set up images of those realities that would have proceeded from the power.' Artists, then, become nothing less than the executors of God's unfinished creation. No wonder Rilke had not bothered his head with arguments about the usefulness or uselessness of art!

Nor had Rilke been shaken in his faith by his reading either of Kierkegaard, with his impassioned insistence on the differences between the aesthetic, moral and spiritual realms, or of Tolstoy's exasperated fulminations against the bourgeois, late Romantic cult of art. Rilke's faith had accommodated all sorts of contradictions, all sorts of opposing influences. He had glorified what looked like military heroism in an early prose poem, and was to do so again at the outbreak of the First World War, even though he saw his own military education as an unmitigated disaster. He had celebrated what looked like Christian piety in his early *Book of Hours*, and was to do so again as late as 1912 in his sequence of poems *The Life of the Virgin Mary* – a sequence he did collect for publication – while remaining committed to a

Nietzschean vitalism and becoming overtly anti-Christian elsewhere. In poems, stories and plays he had contributed to the literature of social compassion, identifying with the poor, oppressed and outcast, but never committed himself politically against the *status quo*, and went out of his way to establish an aristocratic pedigree for himself. And all this with a childlike and genuine innocence, an untroubled candour, even with an aura of Franciscan sanctity for many of his most mundane and sophisticated acquaintances.

One outstanding exception among these was the essayist Rudolf Kassner – himself remarkable for a range that extended from the mundane to the mystical, though with clearly differentiated gradations and a critical acerbity that Rilke was quite capable of, but rarely chose to exercise – and it was Kassner who gave Rilke the epigraph for one of the starkest confessions of his crisis period, the poem 'Turning-Point'. Rilke, who had few male friends, regarded Kassner with an understandable mixture of reverence and awe, since he knew and felt that this fellow guest of Princess Marie's at Duino could see right through his unresolved and previously unacknowledged contradictions. Yet Kassner admired Rilke's work; and Rilke called Kassner 'the only man to whom it has occurred to have a little use for what is feminine in me'. In a retrospective judgement of Rilke, published in 1949, Kassner wrote: 'In Rilke's case one can speak of a sublimated phallicism. Phallicism here amounts to the celebration of a world without original sin, with nothing to replace it in human life but omissions, hastinesses, volatilizations, misses or bunglings.' Kassner is not likely to have known Rilke's sequence *Seven Poems* of 1915, first published in the 1957 edition of Rilke's collected works, which are indeed a quite undisguised celebration of unsublimated phallicism (by all but Rilke's own criterion of aesthetic, metaphorical sublimation); but Kassner did know the Third Duino Elegy, its 'river-god of the blood', its 'Lord of Lust' whose 'godhead' rises and drips. Intimations of original sin and guilt can be detected in the *Elegies*, but not in the *Seven Poems*, with their pervasive imagery of buds (with the woman as 'rose-gatherer' and site of an 'internal garden'), towers, and even cupolas that take off into the woman's 'soft nights' with the 'thrust of womb-dazzling rockets' to hurl into them 'more feeling than I am':

> (um in deine weichen Nächte hin
> mit dem Schwung schooßblendender Raketen
> mehr Gefühl zu schleudern, als ich bin.)

By the time he completed the *Elegies*, in 1922, Rilke had acknowledged this phallicism and made it the basis of his opposition to Christianity. 'The horrible thing,' he wrote to a correspondent in 1922, 'is that we have no religion in which these experiences, as literally and palpably as they are (for at the same time they are so ineffable and unassailable), may be raised up into the god, into the aegis of a phallic deity who may well have to be the first to usher in the return of a divine host amid humankind, after such a long absence.' In the same year Rilke wrote his *Letter of a Young Working Man* – 'Young Artisan' in the published English version, presumably because it seemed inconceivable to the translator that a mere 'working man' could be as articulate and thoughtful as Rilke's *persona* in the letter: 'And here, in that love which with an unbearable combination of contempt, prurience and curiosity they call "sensual", in this perhaps we must look for the worst effects of that condescension with which Christianity thought it necessary to afflict the earthly.' Or again: 'Why have they made our sex homeless, instead of making it the site for the celebration of our responsibility?' Despite everything that Rilke had written about the ruthlessness and coarseness of male sexuality, as compared with the female sexuality that can transcend its object and become pure religious devotion – and Christian devotion specifically – he had arrived at a position closer to that of D. H. Lawrence than to that of Nietzsche, who had done the philosophical and ethical demolition work for both Rilke and Lawrence.

Kassner also remarked of Rilke: 'Seen in a large perspective, he is the consummation of that marvellous Narcissus-like lyricism that began in England with Keats.' That judgement, too, goes straight to the centre of Rilke's crisis, of the circle in which he found himself trapped. On the level of personal life it points to the Narcissus complex of a whole group of poems of the crisis years, of which 'Turning-Point' and the shorter of two poems called 'Narcissus' are included here. Rilke had never stinted praise of women in general, and had made a special cult of those who came up against the limits of sexual love, transmuting it into an early death or into religious dedication; but, before and after a marriage that was suspended indefinitely rather than broken off, despite the birth of a daughter, for the sake of the solitude and freedom that Rilke thought he owed to his vocation, he was unable to commit himself to any one woman for any length of time. The same crisis that cast doubt on this kind of love – a generalized love that could flow anywhere, anyhow, into persons, things, the whole cosmos, animal, vegetable or mineral in Rilke's earlier poems, provided that nothing went out of the poet and he 'never went out of himself' (Baudelaire's definition of the 'dandy' or narcissist) – also cast doubt on Rilke's vocation; such a painful doubt that he considered studying medicine, taking up horse-riding, becoming a country doctor and even submitting to psychoanalysis at this time. 'Perhaps I shall now learn to become a little human' was how he put it to Princess Marie in 1910, with characteristic candour, mildness and wistfulness; but the anguish he suffered at this period was anything but mild. Nor was it squeamishness that made him resist psycho-analysis, and finally recoil from it. (He was quite willing to face up to all his personal weaknesses, erotic or otherwise; and the poem about his mother – p. 65 – is as uninhibited by reticence as any that Robert Lowell was to write about his mother or wives when Freud's theories had become as much part of a life-style as Coca-Cola.) What prevented Rilke from committing himself to treatment was his awareness that his deficiencies as a man were the sustenance of his work; that he must suffer the anguish, pace his circular cage, and put his trust in those transmutations all his work had glorified. In a letter to Lou Andreas-Salomé – his link between Nietzsche, Tolstoy and Freud – written on the very day of his final decision against analysis, he saw his choice as one between 'becoming a little human' and 'ceasing to write'. If he had been really serious about wishing to escape from poetry, he wrote to her, 'then one would have the right to have one's devils exorcized, since in one's daily life they really are nothing but a nuisance and a pain, and if the angels also chanced to be driven out, one would have to see that, too, as a simplification and tell oneself that in one's next profession (which?) they certainly wouldn't be of any use.' Rilke never changed his way of life; but he learned from the crisis, by accepting both his 'phallicism' and his 'femininity', for instance, or by this admission both to himself and to his friend and patron Princess Marie (in a letter of 1913): 'I am no lover at all, it only takes hold of me from outside, perhaps because I do not love my mother. . . . To me, all love is an exertion.' Rilke's narcissism, then, amounted to a kind of hermaphroditic self-sufficiency; and in his poetry it proved self-fertile, too. Merely to understand and accept this oddity brought about an integration very much in evidence in the almost neo-classical serenity of much of his post-crisis verse, including the hundreds of poems he wrote in French right up to the year of his death.

If Rilke's work was the 'consummation' of a development that began with Keats, one pointer to that is Keats's discovery of the 'negative capability' of poets, their chameleon mutability, their need to 'make up one's mind about nothing, to let the mind be a thoroughfare for all thought, not a select party', to have 'no Identity', no fixed character, no fixed opinions. The degree to which Keats's description of the poetic character fits Rilke explains the exasperation of exegetes (less wise than Kassner) who have tried to make sense of the cosmology, ontology or theology that Rilke thought he had enunciated once and for all in the *Elegies* and *Sonnets*, when any statement made in them is a poetic statement valid only within the confines and context of the poetry itself; or, more precisely, when it is a pseudo-philosophical superstructure raised by Rilke on no other foundation than that of poetic *process* – a circular process of perfect reciprocity between the seer and the thing seen, Narcissus and his image in the water. Rilke's glorification of childhood throughout his working life – despite the unhappiness of his own childhood – was another instance of his stubborn clinging to negative capability; and all the contradictions, ambivalences and absurdities of his views on political, social and ethical issues can be understood with the help of Keats's definition. No one can possibly make sense of these on any other level, or tie Rilke down in retrospect to anything like consistent preferences, let alone allegiances. What Rilke avoided in all such matters is the differentiation that would have demanded responsibility for anything beyond his art. Rilke's world remained a fluid one of infinite mutability, interchangeability and openness. 'Art can proceed only from a pure anonymous centre,' he wrote in 1920, meaning not impersonality or disinterestedness but the freedom of the imagination to function without interference or pressure from any extraneous source, selfless only in Keats's sense of being 'continually in for and filling some other body'. Most of Rilke's linguistic innovations – especially his dynamization and neologization of verbs and their prepositions – have to do with this fluidity and interpenetration. A typical instance is his use of the word 'ausgefühlt' in a letter of 1914 – 'felt through', by analogy with 'worked through' or 'thought through'. This 'feeling through' the most diverse material was Rilke's speciality and strength as a poet, his weakness and inadequacy as a man.

II

From 1910 to 1922 Rilke always insisted that he had lost not only his way, but his very ability to write, as in a letter of 1915 to Princess Marie: 'For five years now, ever since *Malte Laurids* closed behind me, I've been standing around as a beginner, though as a beginner who can't begin.' As late as 1920 he wrote to another correspondent: 'As for work, I've done nothing. My heart had stopped like a clock, the pendulum somewhere had collided with the hand of wretchedness and come to a halt.' Rilke cannot be blamed for his reluctance or inability to see that there was something to be said for the collision – a collision, amongst other things, with his own failure to be 'human' and with facts of life he had used only as raw material to be processed in his inward laboratory and transmuted into poetry or prose. Yet where Rilke's earlier verse has become unpalatable for later readers – and much of it has – it is almost always where Rilke's virtuosity of feeling encountered too little resistance from the hard real quiddity of things – and people, for that matter; where, as he confessed in 'Turning-Point', his inwardness had violated them. This was Rilke's peculiar danger – a facility most conspicuous in his multiple rhyming, alliteration, assonance – all of them linking devices that suggest semantic, as well as sonic, affinities – and in the proliferation of simile in his earlier verse.

Except for a brief period during the war, Rilke's workshop never closed down for any length of time, as even the present small selection attests. His uncollected German poems of the period after 1908 – and he wrote about half as many in French – fill more than 500 closely printed pages in Volumes II and VI of the current edition of his collected works. These, admittedly, include dedicatory verse, drafts, fragments and parts of sequences never completed. Yet Rilke's failure to recognize or appreciate the excellence of some of these poems is difficult to understand other than subjectively, in terms of his own loss of faith, his own sense of disjunction and disorientation. Even his criterion of completeness and coherence for collections of poems is a somewhat questionable one, at least in his own case. The *New Poems* are consistent only in being imaginative penetrations of recognizable persons or things; beyond that they function as separate poems, not necessarily 'grand' in the sense of nineteenth-century 'grand opera', 'grand piano sonatas', the Cathedral of Berlin or the gigantic statues of Bismarck erected there and in Hamburg; and such late nineteenth-century notions of grandeur, in any case, seem remote from Rilke's aesthetic, if not his social, sensibility at this point in his development. Some of the *New Poems*, like the admirable

'Orpheus. Eurydice. Hermes', also stand out from the collection as a whole because in form, theme and diction they anticipate the very developments associated with his crisis; and the completed *Elegies*, which are supposed to have resolved the crisis, are as much its product and expression as some of the short poems that Rilke virtually suppressed. It is the *Sonnets to Orpheus*, not the *Duino Elegies*, that are truly a post-crisis work; and they came to Rilke as a gift and a bonus, after all his anguish over the writing of the *Elegies*. Significantly, too, they revert to strict metre and rhyme, mastered with the almost complacent ease which the crisis years had called in question.

These crisis years of Rilke's coincided with unparalleled convulsions in the artistic life of Europe, and of Germany in particular, and there can be no doubt that Rilke was affected by them. Just as Rilke dated the onset of his crisis two years before he had conceived the writing of the *Elegies*, and four years before the outbreak of war, the eruption of new styles like Expressionism in Germany, and their counterparts elsewhere, preceded the political cataclysms. Rilke's concern with the work of three of the early Expressionist poets, Trakl, Heym and Werfel, is documented in his letters. All of them took an apocalyptic view of the state of European civilization. At the same period Rilke's attention was drawn to the work of Hölderlin by his acquaintance with Norbert von Hellingrath, who was editing texts by Hölderlin that had never appeared in their authentic form. The impact on Rilke of this discovery is attested not only in Rilke's letters and his poem on Hölderlin, included here, but in the syntactic structure of several of his crisis poems and passages of the *Elegies* (whose dominantly dactylic rhythm may also derive from Hölderlin's elegiacs and hexameters).

Rilke's attitudes to revolutions in the arts, true, were as ambivalent and shifting as his attitudes, at the same period, to revolutions in politics. In 1915 he wrote to a friend: 'What else is our function but to present grounds for change, purely, greatly and freely, – have we performed it so badly, so half-heartedly, so little convinced and convincing?' But there was all the difference, for Rilke, between 'grounds' for change and the changes themselves, when they came to be carried out. His initial sympathy with the Bavarian revolution of 1918–1919, which he experienced and watched in Munich, can be traced to its vanishing-point in his letters of those years, even though it was a revolution led by intellectuals whose intentions were undoubtedly 'pure, great and free'. One of the leaders, Gustav Landauer, was as vehemently opposed to Marxism as to capitalism, and a fellow admirer of Hölderlin. Rilke had nothing to say about the manner of his killing by the representatives of 'law and order' – the old order. By December 1918 Rilke, though still hopeful, voiced misgivings about the 'political dilettantism' of the revolutionaries – that was their distinction and their dignity – and wrote: 'By revolution, incidentally, I understand the overcoming of abuses in favour of the deepest tradition.' By this time he had also grown critical – and justifiably so – of the Expressionist movement as a whole: 'The Expressionist, that inward man turned explosive, who pours out the lava of his boiling emotions over everything, insisting that the fortuitous shape assumed by the crust is the new, the future, the valid contour of existence, is nothing but a desperate man.' The noisy, bombastic, expletive literature of later Expressionism, with its patent design on a reader's gut responses, is almost certainly the target of Rilke's poem '. . . When will, when will, when will they let it suffice' of 1922 (p. 81).

Throughout the war, whose outbreak he had hailed in poems celebrating 'the god of war' – not much in evidence in the trenches, as even Rilke must have realized to his acute embarrassment not long after their publication – Rilke had less to say about its carnage than about the loss of the personal belongings he had left behind in his Paris flat. 'The worst thing' about the war, for Rilke, was that 'a certain innocence of life, in which, after all, we grew up, will never again exist for any of us', as he wrote to Princess Marie in 1915. Another comment of the same year was that 'the world has fallen into the hands of men'. The 'god of war', evidently, had abdicated or failed.

Though interesting historically, a fuller account and

analysis of Rilke's odd remarks on current affairs would shed little or no light on the poems in question here – or any of his poetry, come to that. By ceasing to earn his living at about the age of thirty – after his early work as a playwright, occasional lecturer, book reviewer, and his brief employment with Rodin – Rilke had virtually dropped out of economic realities, just as he had dropped out of the domestic realities of marriage and fatherhood, or out of the ties of fixed residence and nationality. (The fact of his Austrian nationality was brought home to him again during the war, with the threat of military service.) From 1912 to 1914 alone Rilke stayed in Paris, Venice, Spain, various parts of Germany, including Berlin, Duino on the Adriatic coast, Venice again, and Assisi. As soon as he could, after the war, he left for Switzerland, a country scarcely affected by the war. He felt as much, or as little, at home in Scandinavia, Russia, Spain, and even North Africa as in any German-speaking country or in France. During and immediately after the war his early prose poem on the love and death in action of an aristocratic ancestor, Cornet von Rilke, became a modest best-seller. When his publisher, who had generously subsidized Rilke for years – as did all the noble or wealthy ladies in whose houses Rilke had stayed for long stretches, the anonymous donor (Ludwig Wittgenstein) of a substantial money award to him, and the Swiss patron who provided him with his last home, Muzot – observed to Rilke in 1921 that if all the published 200,000 copies of *Cornet* were placed in a row, it would take a quarter of an hour to walk past them, Rilke's comment, in a letter, was : 'Practical as I am (!), I immediately thought: wouldn't that be a remedy for my cold feet?'

By this time money matters and commercial successes – which had meant a great deal to Rilke in his youth, as his letters to his early publisher Axel Juncker show – had become neither serious nor decent as far as he was concerned; and he also refused a decoration offered to him by the Austrian Government in 1918. In money he saw something like original sin, remarking in a letter of 1914 that it had 'become a thing of the mind or spirit' ('geistig'). Yet money seems to have been redeemed for him as soon as it had been turned into great houses and their rose gardens or works of art, like the Picasso painting with which Rilke lived for months in a borrowed flat, transfiguring it into material for one of the *Elegies* – or when its owners had the 'innocence' of those who do not need to earn it.

When Rilke chose to focus his attention on public events and institutions, as he rarely did, he could be a penetrating critic; so in a letter of August 1915, already quoted here, weighing up the responsibility of the Press for the lying propaganda that kept the war going. Probably he had read the brilliant polemic against it by the theologian Theodor Haecker, published in the same annual issue of *Der Brenner* (1915) to which Rilke contributed a poem, and as devastatingly eloquent as any satire by Karl Kraus. The rubbing off on Rilke of Haecker's Kierkegaardian Christian radicalism in this piece would also explain Rilke's remark in his letter about the world's having 'fallen into the hands of men'. Yet, unlike Haecker's, all Rilke's attitudes and positions lead us back ultimately to his 'negative capability' as a poet, to an aesthetic specialization so intense as to subsume all his seemingly religious, ethical or social concerns.

III

In the present selection from Rilke's miscellaneous poems of the crisis and post-crisis years I have drawn on those in which Rilke confronted energies or realities, whether outward or inward, that endangered his mastery; or – and this often amounts to the same thing – those in which he ventured into territory that was new to him. Some of these poems will seem uncharacteristic to readers who have arrived at a view of Rilke based on his more official canon; but like most major artists Rilke incorporated several minor ones. Rilke's whimsical and mischievous wit, for instance, may be less conspicuous in the official canon than in poems like the one about his mother or in 'Will-o'-the-Wisps', though even the *Elegies* are not as consistently solemn as they have been made out to be. A 'haiku' by Rilke – he wrote another in French, also without observing a syllable count – is included as an instance of his extraordinary formal range and adventurousness, as well as of the miniaturism that counterbalanced any proclivities he may have had to late nineteenth-century monumentalism. Nor have I barred undefinitive or fragmentary pieces, if they promised or intimated more than the numerous finished poems, elegantly rhymed, that Rilke could dash off at all but his very worst moments to keep the wheel turning. For related reasons – rather than the difficulty of translating his rhymed poems without losing the elegance or straying too far from the sense – his poems in free or blank verse preponderate in the selection.

Rilke's personal crisis – to do with a solitude and human unrelatedness taken on by him in the service of his art, and become not only unbearable, but subject to doubts about his own motives and so about the vocation itself – dominates the poems written from 1912 to 1915. These, in fact, were fruitful and crucial years, too, though Rilke could not admit it, intent as he was on a resolution of the crisis and on the completion of the *Elegies* he had begun at Duino in 1912. The *Elegies* were to have resolved the crisis poetically, if not practically, by balancing lament with the praise that Rilke considered the main function of poets and poetry, while conceding that lament, and even satire, might be the reverse, the dark side of the same celebration. 'Pearls roll away . . .' is the first of the stark laments that could not break through into celebration; indeed, it breaks off at the lowest point, where personal weakness, the fear of aging and being displaced (by children!) sets up a barrier of what Rilke must have felt to be almost abject pettiness.

More often though, in these crisis poems, as in the *Elegies* also, Rilke's personal confessions and his existential affirmations or negations are inseparable from questions about the function of poetry and poets. That is so in 'The Spanish Trilogy', 'The Spirit Ariel', 'Turning-Point' and most of the other poems of 1913–1915. 'The Spanish Trilogy' enters into the very processes of poetry, as Rilke experienced them;

complete with his wonderment at the way in which unrelatedness, strangeness, fortuitousness turn into the most intimate self-identification, and even with the awareness – characteristic of his crisis years – that most of his readers will find these processes unacceptable, if not ridiculous, because the poet's self-identification with the Spanish shepherd, or with the 'strange old men' in the hospice, can make no difference to them or to anyone or to anything, except by another empathetic transference – the act of reading. Rilke abjures his magic by letting readers into the mysteries, the secrets and the tricks; and that links 'The Spanish Trilogy' to 'The Spirit Ariel', also written at Ronda in Spain, Rilke's only real tribute to Shakespeare. (Rilke's bizarre aversion to English poetry and the English language, despite Kassner's prompting, was fully documented, investigated and assessed by Eudo C. Mason in *Rilke, Europe and the English-Speaking World*; as late as 1910 Rilke shocked Kassner by declaring that he had never read *Hamlet*!) Ariel, in Rilke's poem, stands for the inspiration that Rilke felt he had lost but Shakespeare appeared to have renounced graciously, if Shakespeare's self-identification with Prospero can be assumed to have been of the same order as Rilke's with Shakespeare and Prospero in this poem.

The Narcissus syndrome has already been touched upon. It is as relevant to 'Turning-Point' as to the little poem called 'Narcissus' – and to a poem not included here, 'Waldteich' (Woodland Pond). The reciprocity of states of mind with what they reflect had been central to Rilke's work since the *Book of Images* and the *Book of Hours*. Multiple and complex interactions or mirrorings occurred in much other poetry of the period, as in that of Paul Valéry, whom Rilke translated. The operative and most uniquely Rilkean line in this brief interpretation of the Narcissus myth is

> Whatever left him he loved back again,

a formidably compact description of the kind of imaginative loving that Rilke could not abjure without giving up poetry; and 'Turning-Point' is the most radical of Rilke's attempts to face up to its cost to him and others on the level of human relationships.

The smooth rhymed iambics of 'Narcissus' – not quite so smooth or regular in my version – enact the reciprocity, which becomes critical in this poem, being tantamount to self-destruction. 'Turning-Point' and 'Complaint', on the other hand, move with a rhythmic and syntactic freedom close to that of early Expressionist verse or to the 'organic form' evolved by Hölderlin for his late visionary poems. The same freedom, like Hölderlin's influence, distinguishes 'Christ's Descent into Hell'. Even without going into the theological implications of Rilke's rendering of the apocryphal Harrowing of Hell, readers of this poem can hardly avoid being struck by its lack of emphasis on judgement. What Rilke's poem stresses and reiterates are suffering and accomplishment – an expertise, a virtuosity in suffering that shames the torments of Hell.

'Complaint' (or 'Lament', as it could have been called) introduces the angels more familiar from the *Duino Elegies*, symbols of transcendence it is wisest to interpret not theologically but poetically, in terms only of Rilke's own system of infinite transmutation and metamorphosis. Much the same power to shatter and to transform is attributed to women in the poem 'A Man Has to Die . . .' (p. 53), as in many poems of Rilke's, because his world is one without hierarchic divisions between the natural and the supernatural. His resistance to such divisions has a bearing on his admiration in early years for what one might call the applied Christianity that impressed him in Russia and on his later sympathy with Islamic devotion. In a letter of 1915 he remarked to Princess Marie: 'For what is it I am seeking so desperately, if not the one point, the Old Testament point, at which the dreadful converges with the utmost greatness'; and he goes on to write: 'For one thing is certain, that the most divine consolation inheres in the human itself: we shouldn't know what to do with the consolation offered by a god; but our eye would have to grow just a little more seeing, our ear more receptive, the flavour of a fruit would have to come home to us more completely, we should be able to bear more smell, and have more presence of mind, be less forgetful, in touching and being touched –; and at once we should derive consolations from our most immediate experiences, consolations more convincing, more preponderant, more true than all the suffering that can shake us.' Rilke's Old Testament poem 'The Death of Moses', written a few months after this letter, is also a search for the point where 'the dreadful converges with the utmost greatness', where the divine and the human meet in a relationship of intimate familiarity at once sensuous and spiritual. Hölderlin, in Rilke's poem to him, is praised for a similar capacity to reduce the distance between Heaven and Earth. Rudolf Kassner, in another essay, pointed out that Rilke never made the transition from the 'world of the Father' to the 'world of the Son', that he remained 'unconverted' in a special sense given to the word by Kassner – and incapable of grasping the full significance of sacrifice. The Kassner epigraph to 'Turning-Point' and the dedication to him of the Eighth Duino Elegy testify to Rilke's awareness of this crux, though his 'turning' never amounted to what Kassner meant by conversion. Such metanoia would have demanded the sacrifice of his poetry, or at least of the kind of poetry at which Rilke excelled. As Rilke's late 'Gong' poems show – he wrote another in French – he continued to explore the borders of sensuous perception, to a point of such refinement that the sensuous seems to fuse with the spiritual.

The ironic, bitter poem 'Death' represents the negative side of Rilke's celebrations, like the related passage about the 'modiste, Madame Lamort' in the Fifth Duino Elegy. The poem is negative about the negation and trivialization of death – which to Rilke meant a corresponding negation and trivialization of life – in the contemporary world. Here death becomes the very reverse of the great event rendered in 'The Death of Moses'.

By 1922, and the fragment beginning 'As long as self-thrown things', Rilke was emerging from the crisis, though that poem is as thorough in its exposure of his poetic weakness – his dangerous facility, rooted in narcissism – as the crisis poems had been of his human ones. In its rhythmic structure, too, and in its self-propelling, self-propagating metaphors, it comes close to reading like a parody of Rilke's own earlier manner. Rilke was never afraid of exposing himself to ridicule, and quite capable of laughing at himself. Even his absurdities and mannerisms were wholly his own, never adopted to impress others or for the sake of being 'different'. The poems of the early 'twenties selected here from a large body of highly accomplished minor verse have a new delicacy, lightness of touch and self-detachment – even a new playfulness in the self-portraiture of 'My shy moon-shadow . . .' and 'Will-o'-the-Wisps'.

The next crisis was Rilke's last, that of his slow death by leukaemia. A last legend, too, was put into circulation, to accord with Rilke's epitaph for himself and his conviction that one should have a death of one's own, just as one has a life of one's own: the legend that his illness was due to being stung by the thorn of a rose. In his last poem, though, the legend plays no part. Rilke's religion of aesthetic contemplation and metamorphosis is put to its ultimate test not in images of the self-sufficient rose but in images of burning, of being consumed by pain; and Rilke rises even to this event, by celebrating it not as his end but as one more transmutation. Touchingly and bravely, he includes notes for a recasting or continuation that will differentiate this last experience from early ones, childhood illnesses that did not disrupt the continuity of selfhood, memory and consciousness. Unlike the epitaph, this parenthetical codicil is not exquisite, finished, or metaphysically suggestive; but it proves beyond doubt that Rilke's existential dedication to art was total and wholehearted even in the face of death, down to a last scruple and discrimination. That was truthfulness, too, and heroism of a kind.

MICHAEL HAMBURGER
Suffolk, January 1980

An Unofficial Rilke

Perlen entrollen. Weh, riß eine der Schnüre?
Aber was hülf es, reih ich sie wieder: du fehlst mir,
starke Schließe, die sie verhielte, Geliebte.

War es nicht Zeit? Wie der Vormorgen den Aufgang,
wart ich dich an, blaß von geleisteter Nacht;
wie ein volles Theater, bild ich ein großes Gesicht,
daß deines hohen mittleren Auftritts
nichts mir entginge. O wie ein Golf hofft ins Offne
und vom gestreckten Leuchtturm
scheinende Räume wirft; wie ein Flußbett der Wüste,
daß es vom reinen Gebirg bestürze, noch himmlisch, der Regen, –
wie der Gefangne, aufrecht, die Antwort des einen
Sternes ersehnt, herein in sein schuldloses Fenster;
wie einer die warmen
Krücken sich wegreißt, daß man sie hin an den Altar
hänge, und daliegt und ohne Wunder nicht aufkann:
siehe, so wälz ich, wenn du nicht kommst, mich zu Ende.

Dich nur begehr ich. Muß nicht die Spalte im Pflaster,
wenn sie, armsälig, Grasdrang verspürt: muß sie den ganzen
Frühling nicht wollen? Siehe, den Frühling der Erde.
Braucht nicht der Mond, damit sich sein Abbild im Dorfteich
fände, des fremden Gestirns große Erscheinung? Wie kann
das Geringste geschehn, wenn nicht die Fülle der Zukunft,
alle vollzählige Zeit, sich uns entgegenbewegt?

Bist du nicht endlich in ihr, Unsägliche? Noch eine Weile,
und ich besteh dich nicht mehr. Ich altere oder dahin
bin ich von Kindern verdrängt . . .

Pearls roll away. Ah, did the string break?
But what use if I restring them: you're lacking,
strong clasp that would hold them in place, beloved one.

Wasn't it time? As first light waits for sunrise
I wait towards you, pale with the effort of it,
getting the better of night;
like a packed theatre I form one large face
lest I should miss one tiniest movement
of your noble entrance mid-stage.
Oh, as an inlet hopes into the open sea
and from the reaching-out lighthouse casts
luminous spaces; or as a desert riverbed,
so that, celestial still, rain from pure mountains shall rush it, –
as the prisoner, upright, yearns for the answer
of the one star, into his innocent window;
as a man will jerk
the warm crutches from under his arms, so that they shall be hung
on the altar, and he lies there and cannot rise
without a miracle: look, that is how
if you do not come, I shall crawl to my ending.

Only you I long for. Must not the crack in the pavement
when, wretched, it senses the surge of grass: must it not
will the whole of spring? The spring of earth.
Does not the moon, so that its image shall find
itself in the village pond, have need of the strange planet's whole
great appearance? How can
the least thing happen unless the future's fulness,
all of time, makes its way towards us, complete?

Are you not in it at last, you whose name I can't speak?
Only a little more holding back,
and I shall fail you, not up to you, aging,
or pushed aside by children to where . . .

1912

DIE SPANISCHE TRILOGIE

I

Aus dieser Wolke, siehe: die den Stern
so wild verdeckt, der eben war – (und mir),
aus diesem Bergland drüben, das jetzt Nacht,
Nachtwinde hat für eine Zeit – (und mir),
aus diesem Fluß im Talgrund, der den Schein
zerrissner Himmels-Lichtung fängt – (und mir);
aus mir und alledem ein einzig Ding
zu machen, Herr: aus mir und dem Gefühl,
mit dem die Herde, eingekehrt im Pferch,
das große dunkle Nichtmehrsein der Welt
ausatmend hinnimmt –, mir und jedem Licht
im Finstersein der vielen Häuser, Herr:
ein Ding zu machen; aus den Fremden, denn
nicht Einen kenn ich, Herr, und mir und mir
ein Ding zu machen; aus den Schlafenden,
den fremden alten Männern im Hospiz,
die wichtig in den Betten husten, aus
schlaftrunknen Kindern an so fremder Brust,
aus vielen Ungenaun und immer mir,
aus nichts als mir und dem, was ich nicht kenn,
das Ding zu machen, Herr Herr Herr, das Ding,
das welthaft-irdisch wie ein Meteor
in seiner Schwere nur die Summe Flugs
zusammennimmt: nichts wiegend als die Ankunft.

II

Warum muß einer gehn und fremde Dinge
so auf sich nehmen, wie vielleicht der Träger
den fremdlings mehr und mehr gefüllten Marktkorb
von Stand zu Stand hebt und beladen nachgeht
und kann nicht sagen: Herr, wozu das Gastmahl?

Warum muß einer dastehn wie ein Hirt,
so ausgesetzt dem Übermaß von Einfluß,

THE SPANISH TRILOGY

I

Out of this cloud – the one that so wildly obscures
the star that was a moment ago – (and me),
out of these mountain regions that now have night,
night breezes for a while at least – (and me),
out of this river in the dell that catches
this torn sky-clearing's brightness now – (and me);
out of all that and out of me to make
a single thing, Lord: me and the sensation
with which the flock, brought back into the pen,
breathe out acceptance of the vast and black
no-longer-being of the world –, me and each light
amid the dark of all these houses, Lord:
to make a thing; and out of strangers, for
not one man I know here, and me and me,
to make *one* thing; out of those now asleep,
the strange old men asleep now in the hospice,
who cough in bed importantly, and out of
sleep-drunken babies at breasts all strange,
out of manifold vagueness and always me,
nothing but me and what I do not know,
to make that thing, O Lord, Lord, Lord, the thing
that cosmic-terrestial like a meteor
concentrates in its gravity the sum total
of flying only, weighs nothing but arrival.

II

Why must a man go out and take strange things
so much upon himself as might the porter
from stall to stall of some large market basket
strangely filled more and more, who, laden, follows
and cannot say: Lord, what's the banquet for?

Why must a man just stand there like a shepherd,
so much exposed to more than he can bear

beteiligt so an diesem Raum voll Vorgang,
daß er gelehnt an einen Baum der Landschaft
sein Schicksal hätte, ohne mehr zu handeln.
Und hat doch nicht im viel zu großen Blick
die stille Milderung der Herde. Hat
nichts als Welt, hat Welt in jedem Aufschaun,
in jeder Neigung Welt. Ihm dringt, was andern
gerne gehört, unwirtlich wie Musik
und blind ins Blut und wandelt sich vorüber.

Da steht er nächtens auf und hat den Ruf
des Vogels draußen schon in seinem Dasein
und fühlt sich kühn, weil er die ganzen Sterne
in sein Gesicht nimmt, schwer –, o nicht wie einer,
der der Geliebten diese Nacht bereitet
und sie verwöhnt mit den gefühlten Himmeln.

III

Daß mir doch, wenn ich wieder der Städte Gedräng
und verwickelten Lärmknäul und die
Wirrsal des Fahrzeugs um mich habe, einzeln,
daß mir doch über das dichte Getrieb
Himmel erinnerte und der erdige Bergrand,
den von drüben heimwärts die Herde betrat.
Steinig sei mir zu Mut
und das Tagwerk des Hirten scheine mir möglich,
wie er einhergeht und bräunt und mit messendem Steinwurf
seine Herde besäumt, wo sie sich ausfranst.
Langsamen Schrittes, nicht leicht, nachdenklichen Körpers,
aber im Stehn ist er herrlich. Noch immer dürfte ein Gott
heimlich in diese Gestalt und würde nicht minder.
Abwechselnd weilt er und zieht, wie selber der Tag,
und Schatten der Wolken
durchgehn ihn, als dächte der Raum
langsam Gedanken für ihn.

of influx, and so much a party to
this space filled with occurrence, that by leaning
against one tree-trunk in that landscape he
would have his fate, without another action.
And yet within his far too open gaze
has not the flock's calm palliation. Has
world, only world, has world in every up-gaze,
in every lowering, world. Into his blood
drives what to others willingly belongs,
to him as inhospitable as music,
and blindly, then transmutes itself, moves past him.

There in the night he rises and already
inside his being has the call of birds
outside, and he feels bold because he takes
all of the stars into his vision, heavy –
O not like one who makes this night a gift
for her he loves and spoils her with felt skies.

III

May to me, though, when once more I have the city's
jostling and tangled clew of noise and
the traffic's turmoil around me, separate,
may to me then over the dense bustle
sky return and the earthy foot of the mountain
which back there homeward the flock ascended.
Stony let me feel then,
and the shepherd's day-labour seem possible,
how he walks about, gets browner, and with a measuring cast
of a stone confines his flock where it straggles.
At a slow pace, not lightly, his body pensive,
but glorious when he stands still. Even now a god in secret
could enter that figure and not be diminished.
Now he lingers, now moves on, as the day does,
and shadows of clouds
pass through him, as though space
slowly for him were thinking thoughts.

Sei er wer immer für euch. Wie das wehende Nachtlicht
in den Mantel der Lampe stell ich mich innen in ihn.
Ein Schein wird ruhig. Der Tod
fände sich reiner zurecht.

You must make of him what you please. Like the wavering night
    light
into the lamp's mantle I place myself in him, inside him.
An effulgence steadies. More purely
death would find its way around.

January 1913

DER GEIST ARIEL

Nach der Lesung von Shakespeares Sturm

Man hat ihn einmal irgendwo befreit
mit jenem Ruck, mit dem man sich als Jüngling
ans Große hinriß, weg von jeder Rücksicht.
Da ward er willens, sieh: und seither dient er,
nach jeder Tat gefaßt auf seine Freiheit.
Und halb sehr herrisch, halb beinah verschämt,
bringt mans ihm vor, daß man für dies und dies
ihn weiter brauche, ach, und muß es sagen,
was man ihm half. Und dennoch fühlt man selbst,
wie alles das, was man mit ihm zurückhält,
fehlt in der Luft. Verführend fast und süß:
ihn hinzulassen –, um dann, nicht mehr zaubernd,
ins Schicksal eingelassen wie die andern,
zu wissen, daß sich seine leichte Freundschaft,
jetzt ohne Spannung, nirgends mehr verpflichtet,
ein Überschuß zu dieses Atmens Raum,
gedankenlos im Element beschäftigt.
Abhängig fürder, länger nicht begabt,
den dumpfen Mund zu jenem Ruf zu formen,
auf den er stürzte. Machtlos, alternd, arm
und doch *ihn* atmend wie unfaßlich weit
verteilten Duft, der erst das Unsichtbare
vollzählig macht. Auflächelnd, daß man dem
so winken durfte, in so großen Umgang
so leicht gewöhnt. Aufweinend vielleicht auch,
wenn man bedenkt, wie's einen liebte und
fortwollte, beides, immer ganz in Einem.

(Ließ ich es schon? Nun schreckt mich dieser Mann,
der wieder Herzog wird. Wie er sich sanft
den Draht ins Haupt zieht und sich zu den andern
Figuren hängt und künftighin das Spiel
um Milde bittet. . . . Welcher Epilog
vollbrachter Herrschaft. Abtun, bloßes Dastehn
mit nichts als eigner Kraft: ›und das ist wenig.‹)

THE SPIRIT ARIEL

After reading Shakespeare's 'The Tempest'

At some time somewhere he was liberated
with such a jerk as being young one used
to rip oneself towards greatness, away from stint.
He willed it then; and ever since has served,
ready for freedom after every deed.
Half very masterfully, half almost embarrassed,
one put it to him that for this and that
he's needed still, oh, and has to tell him
how he was helped. And yet one is aware
how all one uses him to keep away
deprives the air. Almost it's tempting, sweet
to let him go –, and then, abjuring magic,
enrolled in destiny like all the others,
to know his easy friendship from now on,
rid of all tension, of all obligation,
a bonus to the ambit of this breathing,
busies itself in the element at random.
Henceforth dependent, no longer with the gift
of shaping a dull mouth into that call
which brought him down. Powerless, aging, poor,
yet breathing *him* like an impalpably far
fragrance, diffused, by which alone the invisible
becomes complete. And smiling at the thought
that one could summon him so, so lightly lean
on such great intercourse. And weeping too
perhaps to think how then it loved one and
longed to escape, both urges always one.

(Have I released it? Now he frightens me,
this man turned Duke again. How gently now
through his own head he threads the wire and hangs
himself up with the other figures and henceforth
begs the play's indulgence. . . . What an epilogue
to mastery achieved. A stripping, mere standing there
with none but his own strength, 'which is most faint'.)

early 1913

Unwissend vor dem Himmel meines Lebens,
anstaunend steh ich. O die großen Sterne.
Aufgehendes und Niederstieg. Wie still.
Als wär ich nicht. Nehm ich denn Teil? Entriet ich
dem reinen Einfluß? Wechselt Flut und Ebbe
in meinem Blut nach dieser Ordnung? Abtun
will ich die Wünsche, jeden andern Anschluß,
mein Herz gewöhnen an sein Fernstes. Besser
es lebt im Schrecken seiner Sterne, als
zum Schein beschützt, von einer Näh beschwichtigt.

Ignorant I confront the heaven of my life,
wondering at it, I stand. O the great stars.
The rising and the going down. How still.
As though I were not. Am I part of it?
Or have I lost it, severed the pure influx?
Does the same order make
the high and low tides alternate in my blood?
All craving I'll discard, all other connection,
attune my heart to its remotest wave.
Much better to live in terror of its stars
than seemingly pampered, soothed by a nearness.

Spring 1913

[Draft of a poem originally intended for the *Duino Elegies*]

NARZISS

Narziss verging. Von seiner Schönheit hob
sich unaufhörlich seines Wesens Nähe,
verdichtet wie der Duft vom Heliotrop.
Ihm aber war gesetzt, daß er sich sähe.

Er liebte, was ihm ausging, wieder ein
und war nicht mehr im offnen Wind enthalten
und schloß entzückt den Umkreis der Gestalten
und hob sich auf und konnte nicht mehr sein.

NARCISSUS

Narcissus perished. From his beauty rose
incessantly the nearness of his being,
like scent of heliotrope that clings and cloys.
But his one avocation was self-seeing.

Whatever left him he loved back again,
he whom the open wind could not contain;
rapt, closed the round of reciprocity,
annulled himself, and could no longer be.

April 1913

CHRISTI HÖLLENFAHRT

Endlich verlitten, entging sein Wesen dem schrecklichen
Leibe der Leiden. Oben. Ließ ihn.
Und die Finsternis fürchtete sich allein
und warf an das Bleiche
Fledermäuse heran, – immer noch schwankt abends
in ihrem Flattern die Angst vor dem Anprall
an die erkaltete Qual. Dunkle ruhlose Luft
entmutigte sich an dem Leichnam; und in den starken
wachsamen Tieren der Nacht war Dumpfheit und Unlust.
Sein entlassener Geist gedachte vielleicht in der Landschaft
anzustehen, unhandelnd. Denn seiner Leidung Ereignis
war noch genug. Maßvoll
schien ihm der Dinge nächtliches Dastehn,
und wie ein trauriger Raum griff er darüber um sich.
Aber die Erde, vertrocknet im Durst seiner Wunden,
aber die Erde riß auf, und es rufte im Abgrund.
Er, Kenner der Martern, hörte die Hölle
herheulend, begehrend Bewußtsein
seiner vollendeten Not: daß über dem Ende der seinen
(unendlichen) ihre, währende Pein erschrecke, ahne.
Und er stürzte, der Geist, mit der völligen Schwere
seiner Erschöpfung herein: schritt als ein Eilender
durch das befremdete Nachschaun weidender Schatten,
hob zu Adam den Aufblick, eilig,
eilte hinab, schwand, schien und verging in dem Stürzen
wilderer Tiefen. Plötzlich (höher höher) über der Mitte
aufschäumender Schreie, auf dem langen
Turm seines Duldens trat er hervor: ohne Atem,
stand, ohne Geländer, Eigentümer der Schmerzen. Schwieg.

CHRIST'S DESCENT INTO HELL

Beyond it at last, his being escaped from the terrible
body of torments. Above. Left him.
And the dark, all alone, was afraid
and against the pallor
threw bats, in whose nightfall fluttering even now
wavers the fear of colliding
with an anguish grown cold. The dull, restless air
lost courage in face of the corpse; and a listlessness, a distaste
filled the sturdy, wakeful creatures of night.
Dismissed, his spirit perhaps thought of lingering
in the landscape, inactive. For the event of his passion
was still enough. Measured
it seemed to him, the nocturnal standing-there
of things: like a sad space he groped round it.
But the earth, parched in the thirst of his wounds,
but the earth burst open, and something called from the chasm.
He, expert in pains, heard Hell
howl at him, craving awareness
of his accomplished anguish: that through the end of his
(infinite) torture its own, in progress, might be frightened and
    guess.
And he plunged, the spirit, into it with the full weight
of his exhaustion: walked as one hurrying
through the astonished stares of pasturing shades,
raised his gaze to Adam, in haste,
hurried down, vanished, shone and went out in the falling
of wilder depths. All at once (higher, higher) over the midst
of shrieks foaming up, on the tall
tower of his suffering he stepped forth: without breath,
stood with no railing to clutch, agony's owner, in silence.

April 1913

WENDUNG

Der Weg von der Innigkeit zur Größe geht durch das Opfer.
– Kassner

Lange errang ers im Anschaun.
Sterne brachen ins Knie
unter dem ringenden Aufblick.
Oder er anschaute knieend,
und seines Instands Duft
machte ein Göttliches müd,
daß es ihm lächelte schlafend.

Türme schaute er so,
daß sie erschraken:
wieder sie bauend, hinan, plötzlich, in Einem!
Aber wie oft, die vom Tag
überladene Landschaft
ruhete hin in sein stilles Gewahren, abends.

Tiere traten getrost
in den offenen Blick, weidende,
und die gefangenen Löwen
starrten hinein wie in unbegreifliche Freiheit;
Vögel durchflogen ihn grad,
den gemütigen; Blumen
wiederschauten in ihn
groß wie in Kinder.

Und das Gerücht, daß ein Schauender sei,
rührte die minder,
fraglicher Sichtbaren,
rührte die Frauen.

Schauend wie lang?
Seit wie lange schon innig entbehrend,
flehend im Grunde des Blicks?

Wenn er, ein Wartender, saß in der Fremde; des Gasthofs
zerstreutes, abgewendetes Zimmer

TURNING-POINT

The way from intense inwardness to greatness leads through sacrifice.
— Rudolf Kassner

Long he had won it by looking.
Stars would fall on their knees
under his strenuous up-glance.
Or he would look at it kneeling,
and his urgency's odour
made a divine being tired
so that it smiled at him, sleeping.

Towers he would gaze at so
that they were startled:
building them up again, suddenly, sweeping them up!
But how often the landscape
overburdened by day
ebbed to rest in his quiet perceiving, at nightfall.

Animals trustingly stepped
into his open gaze, grazing ones,
even the captive lions
stared in, as though into incomprehensible freedom;
birds flew through it unswerving,
it that could feel them; and flowers
met and returned his gaze,
great as in children.

And the rumour that here was a seeing man
moved the more faintly,
dubiously visible,
moved the women.

Seeing how long?
How long profoundly deprived,
beseeching deep down in his glance?

When he, a waiting one, sat in strange towns; the hotel's
distracted, preoccupied bedroom

mürrisch um sich, und im vermiedenen Spiegel
wieder das Zimmer
und später vom quälenden Bett aus
wieder:
da beriets in der Luft,
unfaßbar beriet es
über sein fühlbares Herz,
über sein durch den schmerzhaft verschütteten Körper
dennoch fühlbares Herz
beriet es und richtete:
daß es der Liebe nicht habe.

(Und verwehrte ihm weitere Weihen.)

Denn des Anschauns, siehe, ist eine Grenze.
Und die geschautere Welt
will in der Liebe gedeihn.

Werk des Gesichts ist getan,
tue nun Herz-Werk
an den Bildern in dir, jenen gefangenen; denn du
überwältigtest sie: aber nun kennst du sie nicht.
Siehe, innerer Mann, dein inneres Mädchen,
dieses errungene aus
tausend Naturen, dieses
erst nur errungene, nie
noch geliebte Geschöpf.

morose about him, and in the avoided mirror
that room once more
and later, from the tormenting bedstead
once more:
then in the air it pronounced,
beyond his grasping pronounced
on his heart that was still to be felt,
through his painfully buried body,
on his heart nonetheless to be felt,
something pronounced then, and judged:
that it was lacking in love.

(And forbade him further communions.)

For looking, you see, has a limit.
And the more looked-at world
wants to be nourished by love.

Work of seeing is done,
now practise heart-work
upon those images captive within you; for you
overpowered them only: but now do not know them.
Look, inward man, look at your inward maiden,
her the laboriously won
from a thousand natures, at her the
being till now only
won, never yet loved.

June 1914

KLAGE

Wem willst du klagen, Herz? Immer gemiedener
ringt sich dein Weg durch die unbegreiflichen
Menschen. Mehr noch vergebens vielleicht,
da er die Richtung behält,
Richtung zur Zukunft behält,
zu der verlorenen.

Früher. Klagtest? Was wars? Eine gefallene
Beere des Jubels, unreife.
Jetzt aber bricht mir mein Jubel-Baum,
bricht mir im Sturme mein langsamer
Jubel-Baum.
Schönster in meiner unsichtbaren
Landschaft, der du mich kenntlicher
machtest Engeln, unsichtbaren.

COMPLAINT

To whom, heart, would you complain? Ever more unfrequented
your way grapples on through incomprehensible
human kind. All the more vainly perhaps
for keeping to its direction,
direction towards the future,
the future that's lost.

Before. You complained? What was it? A fallen
berry of joy, an unripe one.
But now it's my tree of joy that is breaking,
what breaks in the gale is my slow
tree of joy.
Loveliest in my invisible
landscape, you that brought me more close to the
ken of angels, invisible.

July 1914

›MAN MUSS STERBEN WEIL MAN SIE KENNT‹
›Papyrus Prisse‹. Aus den Sprüchen des Ptah-hetep, Handschrift um 2000 v. Ch.

›Man muß sterben weil man sie kennt.‹ Sterben
an der unsäglichen Blüte des Lächelns. Sterben
an ihren leichten Händen. Sterben
an Frauen.

Singe der Jüngling die tödlichen,
wenn sie ihm hoch durch den Herzraum
wandeln. Aus seiner blühenden Brust
sing er sie an:
unerreichbare! Ach, wie sie fremd sind.
Über den Gipfeln
seines Gefühls gehn sie hervor und ergießen
süß verwandelte Nacht ins verlassene
Tal seiner Arme. Es rauscht
Wind ihres Aufgangs im Laub seines Leibes. Es glänzen
seine Bäche dahin.

Aber der Mann
schweige erschütterter. Er, der
pfadlos die Nacht im Gebirg
seiner Gefühle geirrt hat:
schweige.

Wie der Seemann schweigt, der ältere,
und die bestandenen
Schrecken spielen in ihm wie in zitternden Käfigen.

'A MAN HAS TO DIE OF KNOWING THEM'

'Papyrus Prisse'. From the sayings of Ptah-hetep. Manuscript circa 2000 B.C.

'A man has to die of knowing them.' Die
of their smile's unspeakable blossom. Die
of their light hands. Die
of women.

Let the young man sing those deadly ones
when high up through his heart-room
they pass. From his blossoming chest
let him sing to them:
inaccessible ones! Oh, how strange they are.
Above the peaks
of his feeling they rise and pour
sweetly transmuted night into the desolate
dale of his arms. The wind
of their rising rustles in leaves of his body. Its brooks
glisten away.

But let the man
be silent more shakenly. Him
who pathless has strayed
on his feeling's last ranges:
be silent.

As the sailor is silent, the older one,
and the terrors that did not kill him
play in him as in tremulous cages.

July 1914

Ausgesetzt auf den Bergen des Herzens. Siehe, wie klein dort,
siehe: die letzte Ortschaft der Worte, und höher,
aber wie klein auch, noch ein letztes
Gehöft von Gefühl. Erkennst du's?
Ausgesetzt auf den Bergen des Herzens. Steingrund
unter den Händen. Hier blüht wohl
einiges auf; aus stummem Absturz
blüht ein unwissendes Kraut singend hervor.
Aber der Wissende? Ach, der zu wissen begann
und schweigt nun, ausgesetzt auf den Bergen des Herzens.
Da geht wohl, heilen Bewußtseins,
manches umher, manches gesicherte Bergtier,
wechselt und weilt. Und der große geborgene Vogel
kreist um der Gipfel reine Verweigerung. – Aber
ungeborgen, hier auf den Bergen des Herzens . . . .

Abandoned bare on the heart's mountains. Look, how small there,
look: the last little village of words, and higher,
but also how small, a last
homestead of feeling. Familiar to you?
Abandoned bare on the heart's mountains. Rock base
under your hands. True, something blossoms
here; from silent erosion
an unknowing herb breaks into blossom, singing.
But the knowing man? He who began to know
and is silent now, abandoned bare on the heart's mountains.
True, with awareness intact many a creature
moves about, many a mountain animal lives secure,
changes and stays. And the great bird at home here
circles the pure negation of peaks. – But
homeless here on the heart's mountains . . .

September 1914

AN HÖLDERLIN

Verweilung, auch am Vertrautesten nicht,
ist uns gegeben; aus den erfüllten
Bildern stürzt der Geist zu plötzlich zu füllenden; Seen
sind erst im Ewigen. Hier ist Fallen
das Tüchtigste. Aus dem gekonnten Gefühl
überfallen hinab ins geahndete, weiter.

Dir, du Herrlicher, war, dir war, du Beschwörer, ein ganzes
Leben das dringende Bild, wenn du es aussprachst,
die Zeile schloß sich wie Schicksal, ein Tod war
selbst in der lindesten, und du betratest ihn; aber
der vorgehende Gott führte dich drüben hervor.

O du wandelnder Geist, du wandelndster! Wie sie doch alle
wohnen im warmen Gedicht, häuslich, und lang
bleiben im schmalen Vergleich. Teilnehmende. Du nur
ziehst wie der Mond. Und unten hellt und verdunkelt
deine nächtliche sich, die heilig erschrockene Landschaft,
die du in Abschieden fühlst. Keiner
gab sie erhabener hin, gab sie ans Ganze
heiler zurück, unbedürftiger. So auch
spieltest du heilig durch nicht mehr gerechnete Jahre
mit dem unendlichen Glück, als wär es nicht innen, läge
keinem gehörend im sanften
Rasen der Erde umher, von göttlichen Kindern verlassen.
Ach, was die Höchsten begehren, du legtest es wunschlos
Baustein auf Baustein: es stand. Doch selber sein Umsturz
irrte dich nicht.

Was, da ein solcher, Ewiger, war, mißtraun wir
immer dem Irdischen noch? Statt am Vorläufigen ernst
die Gefühle zu lernen für welche
Neigung, künftig im Raum?

TO HÖLDERLIN

To stay, among things most familiar even,
we are not permitted; from the image fulfilled
our minds too suddenly rush into those to be filled; there are
no lakes till eternity. Here
falling's the best we can do: tumble over
from the mastered feeling into the guessed at, onward.

To you, glorious one, who adjured it, for you a whole life
was the urgent image, when you pronounced it
the line closed like a fate, in your gentlest even
a death inhered and you entered it; but
the god walking ahead led you out and across.

You roaming spirit, more roaming than any! How all those others
are at home in their snug, warm poems, house-proud, and linger
in narrow analogies. Interested parties. You only
move like the moon. And, below, it lights up and darkens,
your nocturnal landscape, the sacredly startled
which through leave-taking you perceive. No one
gave it away more nobly, gave it back
to the whole more undamaged, more undemandingly. So
too for years no longer counted devoutly you played
with infinite joy, as though it were not inside us
but, belonging to none, lay about
in the tender grass of this earth, left behind by celestial children.
Oh, what the best aspire to, you, undesiring, laid
brick upon brick: it stood up. But its very collapse
left you composed.

How, after one so timeless has been, can we
still mistrust the earthly? Rather than earnestly learning
from provisional things the feelings for what
inclination to come, in space?

September 1914

Immer wieder, ob wir der Liebe Landschaft auch kennen
und den kleinen Kirchhof mit seinen klagenden Namen
und die furchtbar verschweigende Schlucht, in welcher die andern
enden: immer wieder gehn wir zu zweien hinaus
unter die alten Bäume, lagern uns immer wieder
zwischen die Blumen, gegenüber dem Himmel.

Again and again, though we know the landscape of love
and the little graveyard with its lamenting names
and the terrible reticent gorge in which the others
end: again and again we go out in couples
under the ancient trees, lie down again and again
among the wild flowers, facing the sky.

Autumn 1914

DER TOD MOSES

Keiner, der finstere nur gefallene Engel
wollte; nahm Waffen, trat tödlich
den Gebotenen an. Aber schon wieder
klirrte er hin rückwärts, aufwärts,
schrie in die Himmel: Ich kann nicht!

Denn gelassen durch die dickichte Braue
hatte ihn Moses gewahrt und weitergeschrieben:
Worte des Segens und den unendlichen Namen.
Und sein Auge war rein bis zum Grunde der Kräfte.

Also der Herr, mitreißend die Hälfte der Himmel,
drang herab und bettete selber den Berg auf;
legte den Alten. Aus der geordneten Wohnung
rief er die Seele; die, auf! und erzählte
vieles Gemeinsame, eine unzählige Freundschaft.

Aber am Ende wars ihr genug. Daß es genug sei,
gab die vollendete zu. Da beugte der alte
Gott zu dem Alten langsam sein altes
Antlitz. Nahm ihn im Kusse aus ihm
in sein Alter, das ältere. Und mit Händen der Schöpfung
grub er den Berg zu. Daß es nur einer,
ein wiedergeschaffener, sei unter den Bergen der Erde,
Menschen nicht kenntlich.

THE DEATH OF MOSES

Not one who wanted glory and only fallen
angels; took weapons, deadly approached
the commanded man. But already
He clanked back again, upward,
roared out into the heavens: I cannot!

For calmly through his thickety eyebrows
Moses had seen Him and written on:
words of blessing and the infinite name.
And his eye was pure down to the bedrock of powers.

So the Lord, half the heavens swept up in the motion,
plunged and Himself made a couch of the mountain;
laid the old man down. From the house set in order
He called the soul; it was up and telling
many a tale of things shared, of measureless friendship.

But at last it had had enough. That it was enough
the made-perfect admitted. Then the ancient
God to the ancient man slowly inclined
His ancient face. In a kiss took him
into His age, the older. And with hands of creation
He closed the mountain. So that only the one,
one recreated, should lie under terrestial mountains,
unknowable to mankind.

October 1915

DER TOD

Da steht der Tod, ein bläulicher Absud
in einer Tasse ohne Untersatz.
Ein wunderlicher Platz für eine Tasse:
steht auf dem Rücken einer Hand. Ganz gut
erkennt man noch an dem glasierten Schwung
den Bruch des Henkels. Staubig. Und: ›*Hoff-nung*‹
an ihrem Bug in aufgebrauchter Schrift.

Das hat der Trinker, den der Trank betrifft,
bei einem fernen Frühstück ab-gelesen.

Was sind denn das für Wesen,
die man zuletzt wegschrecken muß mit Gift?

Blieben sie sonst? Sind sie denn hier vernarrt
in dieses Essen voller Hindernis?
Man muß ihnen die harte Gegenwart
ausnehmen, wie ein künstliches Gebiß.
Dann lallen sie. Gelall, Gelall . . . .
. . . .

O Sternenfall,
von einer Brücke einmal eingesehn –:
Dich nicht vergessen. Stehn!

DEATH

Here you have death, a bluish decoction
in a cup without a saucer.
A very strange place for a cup:
it stands on the back of a hand. Quite easily
you can make out on the glazed roundness
where the handle broke off. Dusty. And *'ho-pe'*
inscribed on its curve in faded letters.

That word the drinker whom the drink concerns
read off at a breakfast that's remote.

What sort of creatures are these
whom in the end one has to scare off with poison?

Would they stay else? Here, are they so infatuated
with this meal full of hitches?
You have to take hard reality
out of them, like a set of false teeth.
Then they begin to babble: babba, lalla . . . .
. . . .

O fall of stars,
seen from a footbridge once, and scanned:
Never may I forget you. Stand!

November 1915

Ach wehe, meine Mutter reißt mich ein.
Da hab ich Stein auf Stein zu mir gelegt,
und stand schon wie ein kleines Haus, um das sich groß der Tag
    bewegt,
sogar allein.
Nun kommt die Mutter, kommt und reißt mich ein.

Sie reißt mich ein, indem sie kommt und schaut.
Sie sieht es nicht, daß einer baut.
Sie geht mir mitten durch die Wand von Stein.
Ach wehe, meine Mutter reißt mich ein.

Die Vögel fliegen leichter um mich her.
Die fremden Hunde wissen: das ist *der*.
Nur einzig meine Mutter kennt es nicht,
mein langsam mehr gewordenes Gesicht.

Von ihr zu mir war nie ein warmer Wind.
Sie lebt nicht dorten, wo die Lüfte sind.
Sie liegt in einem hohen Herz-Verschlag
und Christus kommt und wäscht sie jeden Tag.

Graue Liebesschlangen hab ich aus deinen
Achselhöhlen gescheucht. Wie auf heißen Steinen
liegen sie jetzt auf mir und verdauen
Lust-Klumpen

Oh, misery, my mother tears me down.
Stone upon stone I'd laid, towards a self
and stood like a small house, with day's expanse around it,
even alone.
Now comes my mother, comes and tears me down.

She tears me down by coming and by looking.
That someone builds she does not see.
Right through my wall of stones she walks for me.
Oh, misery, my mother tears me down.

Birds overhead more lightly fill my space.
Strange dogs can sense it: this one's *that* and *so*.
Only my mother does not know
my oh how slowly incremented face.

From her to me no warm breeze ever blew.
Never she lived where any wind can stir.
In a high glory-hole she likes to lie
and daily Jesus comes and washes her.

October 1915

Grey love-snakes I drove out of your
armpits. As on hot stones
they lie on top of me now, digesting
great lumps of satisfied lust

1915?

Nicht daß uns, da wir (plötzlich) erwachsen sind
und plötzlich mit-schuldig an unvor-
denklicher Schuld der Erwachsenen; Mitwisser plötzlich
aller Gewissen –, nicht daß uns dann ein Häscher errät
und handfest hinüber zerrt und zurück
ins vergangne Gefängnis, wo von der Zeit nur
Abwässer sind, die weggeschüttete Zukunft,
draus eine Welle manchmal mit fast ihm
entgangener Hand der Gefangene aufhebt, sie über den kahlge-
schorenen Kopf hinschüttend wie irgendein Kommen,
----

das nicht [ist unser Ärgstes,]; sondern die Kerker von früh an
die sich aus unserem Atem bilden, aus einer zu zeitig
verstandenen Hoffnung, aus selber
unserem Schicksal. Aus der noch eben
rein durchdringlichen offenen Luft, aus jedem Geschauten.

Wie so mag ein Mädchen auf einmal durch Gitter
seiner Noch-Kindheit den Liebbaren sehn, getrennter
als in Legende. Ihm gegenüber
aufschaun, um ins Vorfrauliche traurig
abzugleiten von ihm.
Oder Getrennten sind mehr. Jahrzehnt und Jahrtausend
von Gesicht zu Gesicht. Und zwischen Erkannten
steht vielleicht im Kerker der Kindheit das besser,
das unendlich berechtigte Herz.

[Mann, sei wie ein Engel,
wenn die Begegnung geschieht und es geht noch das Mädchen
eingelassen einher im Gleichnis der Kindheit.
[Nicht ein Begehrender, welcher bestünde]
Sei wie ein Engel. Laß sie nicht rückwärts. Weiter
gieb ihr die Freiheit. Über das bloße
Lieben gieb ihr die Gnade der Liebe. Bewußtsein

Not that, when (suddenly) we are grown-up
and suddenly share the immemorial
guilt of the grown-up; conniving, suddenly,
in everyone's conscience –, not that then a bailiff suspects us
and by force drags us over and back
to the past prison cell, where there's nothing of time
but its effluents, a future poured down the drain
from which the prisoner with a hand that's almost escaped him
scoops a wavelet from time to time, letting it run
over his shaven head like something that's happening,
———————————————————
not *that* [is our worst]; but the cells from an early age
that form out of our breathing, out of a
hope too soon understood, out of our very
destinies. Out of the only a moment ago
still purely penetrable open air, out of everything looked at.

So might a girl all at once through the bars of her
childhood not yet outgrown catch sight of a
lovable one, more separate than in legends.
Facing him, look up, to slide off him sadly
into pre-womanhood.
O there are more so separate. Decade, millennium
between face and face. And between those who know each other
still in the cell of childhood they could be lying,
their more, their endlessly justified hearts.

[Man, be like an angel
when the encounter occurs and the girl walks about
still mirrored in her childhood's metaphor.
[Not a desiring one out to win.]
Be like an angel. Don't leave her behind you. Continue
to give her that freedom. Beyond
mere loving give her the mercy of love. Give her

gieb ihr der Ströme. Kühnheit der Himmel
stürze um sie. Durch den empfundenen Herzraum
wirf ihr die Vögel]
[Kerker unsägliche, unvermutete Kerker]

AN DIE MUSIK

Musik: Atem der Statuen. Vielleicht:
Stille der Bilder. Du Sprache wo Sprachen
enden. Du Zeit,
die senkrecht steht auf der Richtung vergehender Herzen.

Gefühle zu wem? O du der Gefühle
Wandlung in was? –: in hörbare Landschaft.
Du Fremde: Musik. Du uns entwachsener
Herzraum. Innigstes unser,
das, uns übersteigend, hinausdrängt, –
heiliger Abschied:
da uns das Innre umsteht
als geübteste Ferne, als andre
Seite der Luft:
rein,
riesig,
nicht mehr bewohnbar.

awareness of rivers. Around her heap the
boldness of skies. Through the heart-space perceived
throw her the birds]
[Cells unspeakable, unexpected cells]

Fragments of an elegy, early 1916

TO MUSIC

Music: breathing of statues. Perhaps
stillness of pictures. You language where languages
end. You time
that stands perpendicular on the course of transient hearts.

Feelings for whom? O you the mutation
of feelings to what? –: to audible landscape.
You stranger: music. You heart-space
grown out of us. Innermost of us
that, rising above us, seeks the way out –
holy departure:
when what is inward surrounds us
as the most mastered distance, as
the other side of the air:
pure,
immense,
beyond habitation.

January 1918

Wunderliches Wort: die Zeit vertreiben!
Sie zu *halten*, wäre das Problem.
Denn, wen ängstigts nicht: wo ist ein Bleiben,
wo ein endlich *Sein* in alledem? –

Sieh, der Tag verlangsamt sich, entgegen
jenem Raum, der ihn nach Abend nimmt:
Aufstehn wurde Stehn, und Stehn wird Legen,
und das willig Liegende verschwimmt –

Berge ruhn, von Sternen überprächtigt; –
aber auch in ihnen flimmert Zeit.
Ach, in meinem wilden Herzen nächtigt
obdachlos die Unvergänglichkeit.

HAÏ-KAÏ

Kleine Motten taumeln schauernd quer aus dem Buchs;
sie sterben heute Abend und werden nie wissen,
daß es nicht Frühling war.

To pass the time, to kill it: curious saying!
How *hold* it? the question ought to be.
It racks us all: where, where is there a staying,
where in all this a being finally? –

Look how the day slows down now, on its way
towards the space that takes it into night:
rising soon was to stand, standing to lay;
and that which willingly lies drifts out of sight –

These mountains rest, by higher stars outsplendoured –
yet twinkling there is time again no less.
Oh, to my wild heart comes the re-engendered,
always unhoused imperishableness.

I, 10 of the sequence 'From the Literary Remains of Count C.W.', 1919

HAIKU

Little moths stagger quivering out of the box hedge;
they will die tonight and will never know
that spring had not yet come.

1920

DIE HAND

Siehe die kleine Meise,
hereinverirrte ins Zimmer:
zwanzig Herzschläge lang
lag sie [in] einer Hand.
Menschenhand. Einer zu schützen entschlossenen.
Unbesitzend beschützenden.
Aber
jetzt auf dem Fensterbrett
frei
bleibt sie noch immer im Schrecken
sich selber
und dem Umgebenden fremd,
dem Weltall, erkennts nicht.
Ach so beirrend ist Hand
selbst noch im Retten.
In der beiständigsten Hand
ist noch Todes genug
und war Geld

THE HAND

Look at the little titmouse,
astray in this room:
twenty heartbeats long
it lay within my hand.
Human hand. One resolved to protect.
Unpossessing protect.
But
now on the window-sill
free
in its fear it remains
estranged
from itself and what surrounds it,
the cosmos, unrecognizing.
Ah, so confusing a hand is
even when out to save.
In the most helpful of hands
there is death enough still
and there has been money

1921

GEGEN-STROPHEN

Oh, daß ihr hier, Frauen, einhergeht,
hier unter uns, leidvoll,
nicht geschonter als wir und dennoch imstande,
selig zu machen wie Selige.

Woher,
wenn der Geliebte erscheint,
nehmt ihr die Zukunft?
Mehr, als je sein wird.
Wer die Entfernungen weiß
bis zum äußersten Fixstern,
staunt, wenn er diesen gewahrt,
euern herrlichen Herzraum.
Wie, im Gedräng, spart ihr ihn aus?
Ihr, voll Quellen und Nacht.

Seid ihr wirklich die gleichen,
die, da ihr Kind wart,
unwirsch im Schulgang
anstieß der ältere Bruder?
Ihr Heilen.

    Wo wir als Kinder uns schon
    häßlich für immer verzerrn,
    wart ihr wie Brot vor der Wandlung.

Abbruch der Kindheit
war euch nicht Schaden. Auf einmal
standet ihr da, wie im Gott
plötzlich zum Wunder ergänzt.

    Wir, wie gebrochen vom Berg,
    oft schon als Knaben scharf
    an den Rändern, vielleicht
    manchmal glücklich behaun;
    wir, wie Stücke Gesteins,
    über Blumen gestürzt.

ANTISTROPHES

Oh, that you walk about, women,
here in our midst, suffering,
not more spared than we are, yet able
to grant bliss like the blessed.

Where,
when your loved one appears,
do you find so much future?
More than will ever be.
One who knows the distances
up to the farthest of fixed stars
marvels when he observes it,
this your glorious heart-space.
How, in the bustle, do you leave it open?
You, full of wellsprings and night.

Are you really the same
whom as children,
going to school, your big brothers
gruffly barged into, pushed?
You hale ones.

    Where already as children
    we hideously warp for ever,
    you were like bread before changing.

Childhood's breaking-off
did you no harm. All at once
you stood there, completed
as in a god, to a miracle.

    We, as though chipped from the mountain,
    often as boys even sharp
    at the edges, at times
    perhaps happily hewn;
    we, like bits of rock
    hurled on to flowers.

Blumen des tieferen Erdreichs,
von allen Wurzeln geliebte,
ihr, der Eurydike Schwestern,
immer voll heiliger Umkehr
hinter dem steigenden Mann.

   Wir, von uns selber gekränkt,
   Kränkende gern und gern
   Wiedergekränkte aus Not.
   Wir, wie Waffen, dem Zorn
   neben den Schlaf gelegt.

Ihr, die ihr beinah Schutz seid, wo niemand
schützt. Wie ein schattiger Schlafbaum
ist der Gedanke an euch
für die Schwärme des Einsamen.

Wir, in den ringenden Nächten,
wir fallen von Nähe zu Nähe;
und wo die Liebende taut,
sind wir ein stürzender Stein.

Flowers of the deeper earth levels,
loved by all roots,
you, Eurydice's sisters,
always full of holy conversion
behind the ascending man.

    We, hurt by ourselves,
    keen to hurt and keen
    to be hurt in return in our neediness.
    We, like weapons laid
    beside sleep, for anger.

You that are almost protection, where no one
protects. Like a shady sleep-tree
is the thought of you
for the crowds of lonely men.

We, in the grappling nights,
we fall from nearness to nearness;
and where the loving girl thaws
we hurtle down, stones.

1912–1922

Mein scheuer Mondschatten spräche gern
mit meinem Sonnenschatten von fern
in der Sprache der Toren;
mitten drin ich, ein beschienener Sphinx,
Stille stiftend, nach rechts und links
hab ich die beiden geboren.

My shy moon-shadow would like to talk
with a sun-shadow from afar
in the language of fools;
between them, myself, a sphinx in full light,
endower of stillness, to the left and the right
I've given birth to that pair.

February 1922

... Wann wird, wann wird, wann wird es genügen
das Klagen und Sagen? Waren nicht Meister im Fügen
menschlicher Worte gekommen? Warum die neuen Versuche?

Sind nicht, sind nicht, sind nicht vom Buche
die Menschen geschlagen wie von fortwährender Glocke?
Wenn dir, zwischen zwei Büchern, schweigender Himmel
    erscheint: frohlocke . . .,
oder ein Ausschnitt einfacher Erde im Abend.

Mehr als die Stürme, mehr als die Meere haben
die Menschen geschrieen . . . Welche Übergewichte von Stille
müssen im Weltraum wohnen, da uns die Grille
hörbar blieb, uns schreienden Menschen. Da uns die Sterne
schweigende scheinen, im angeschrieenen Äther!

Redeten uns die fernsten, die alten und ältesten Väter!
Und wir: Hörende endlich! Die ersten hörenden Menschen.

. . . When will, when will, when will they let it suffice,
the complaining, explaining? Have we not had masters to splice
human words, compose them? Why all this new endeavour?

Do not, do not, do not books for ever
hammer at people like perpetual bells?
When, between two books, silent sky appears: be glad . . .,
or a patch of plain earth in the evening.

Louder than gale, louder than sea swell, men
have roared and yelled . . . What preponderances of stillness
must reside in the cosmic spaces, when
the cricket is audible still to yelling mankind.
When stars, the silent, shine for us in the yelled-at heavens!

Oh, if they spoke to us, the remotest, ancient, most ancient
    forebears!
And we: listeners at last. The first human listeners.

1922

Solang du Selbstgeworfnes fängst, ist alles
Geschicklichkeit und läßlicher Gewinn –;
erst wenn du plötzlich Fänger wirst des Balles,
den eine ewige Mit-Spielerin
dir zuwarf, deiner Mitte, in genau
gekonntem Schwung, in einem jener Bögen
aus Gottes großem Brücken-Bau:
erst dann ist Fangen-Können ein Vermögen, –
nicht deines, einer Welt. Und wenn du gar
zurückzuwerfen Kraft und Mut besäßest,
nein, wunderbarer: Mut und Kraft vergäßest
und schon geworfen *hättest* . . . . . (wie das Jahr
die Vögel wirft, die Wandervogelschwärme,
die eine ältre einer jungen Wärme
hinüberschleudert über Meere –) erst
in diesem Wagnis spielst du gültig mit.
Erleichterst dir den Wurf nicht mehr; erschwerst
dir ihn nicht mehr. Aus deinen Händen tritt
das Meteor und rast in seine Räume . . .

As long as self-thrown things you catch, it's all
mere virtuosity, a venial winning –:
not till you find that you have caught the ball
a constant fellow player, she, sent spinning
at you, your centre, one of those throws
precisely angled, mastered, such
as God, the great bridge-builder, knows,
will catching be a skill that counts for much, –
not your skill, but a world's. And if at length
you had the strength and courage for replying,
no, better still, forgot your courage, strength
and had *already* thrown . . . (as does the year,
throwing the birds, a myriad migrant swarm
which older warmth to newer warmth sends flying
across the oceans –) only in that venture,
a valid player, you'd be joining in.
No longer would make it easy for yourself,
no longer difficult. Launched from your hands
into its spaces the meteor would spin . . .

1922

Wir sind nur Mund. Wer singt das ferne Herz,
das heil inmitten aller Dinge weilt?
Sein großer Schlag ist in uns eingeteilt
in kleine Schläge. Und sein großer Schmerz
ist, wie sein großer Jubel, uns zu groß.
So reißen wir uns immer wieder los
und sind nur Mund. Aber auf einmal bricht
der große Herzschlag heimlich in uns ein,
so daß wir schrein –,
und sind dann Wesen, Wandlung und Gesicht.

We're mouths, no more. Who sings the distant heart
that, whole and hale, inheres within all things?
Its mighty beat into small hammerings
in us has been spaced out. So, too, the smart,
the pain – too great for us, like its great joy.
So we tear loose from it repeatedly
and are mere mouth. But right into our fleeing
bursts that great heartbeat, unpredictable,
so that we yell –,
becoming visage, transformation, being.

September 1923

IMAGINÄRER LEBENSLAUF

Erst eine Kindheit, grenzenlos und ohne
Verzicht und Ziel. O unbewußte Lust.
Auf einmal Schrecken, Schranke, Schule, Frohne
und Absturz in Versuchung und Verlust.

Trotz. Der Gebogene wird selber Bieger
und rächt an anderen, daß er erlag.
Geliebt, gefürchtet, Retter, Ringer, Sieger
und Überwinder, Schlag auf Schlag.

Und dann allein im Weiten, Leichten, Kalten.
Doch tief in der errichteten Gestalt
ein Atemholen nach dem Ersten, Alten . . .

Da stürzte Gott aus seinem Hinterhalt.

FICTITIOUS BIOGRAPHY

At first a childhood, boundless, with no aim,
no self-denial. O unconscious bliss.
Then sudden terror, school and rules and shame,
constraint, temptation, fall into otherness.

Defiance. Now the bent becomes the bender,
makes others pay in kind for his defeat.
Loved, feared, a champion, friend, defender,
bully and conqueror, to beat and beat.

Then on his own in cold, wide, weightless air.
Yet deep within the second self's redoubt
a taking breath for what at first was there . . .

When from His ambush God came rushing out.

September 1923

DER MAGIER

Er ruft es an. Es schrickt zusamm und steht.
Was steht? Das Andre; alles, was nicht er ist,
wird Wesen. Und das ganze Wesen dreht
ein raschgemachtes Antlitz her, das mehr ist.

Oh Magier, halt aus, halt aus, halt aus!
Schaff Gleichgewicht. Steh ruhig auf der Waage,
damit sie einerseits dich und das Haus
und drüben jenes Angewachsne trage.

Entscheidung fällt. Die Bindung stellt sich her.
Er weiß, der Anruf überwog das Weigern.
Doch sein Gesicht, wie mit gedeckten Zeigern,
hat Mitternacht. Gebunden ist auch er.

THE MAGICIAN

He calls to it. It twitches, jumps, and stands.
What stands? The other, all that is not he,
materializes. And it turns to him
a face that's more, assembled instantly.

Magician, O hold out, hold out, hold out!
Create an equilibrium. Keep still
the scales that here will bear you and your house,
there, the accreted otherness. Until

decision comes. The fusion has been found.
He knows, conjúring has outweighed denial.
And yet his features, like a covered dial
make the time midnight. Even he is bound.

February 1924

IRRLICHTER

Wir haben einen alten Verkehr
mit den Lichtern im Moor.
Sie kommen mir wie Großtanten vor . . .
Ich entdecke mehr und mehr

zwischen ihnen und mir den Familienzug,
den keine Gewalt unterdrückt:
diesen Schwung, diesen Sprung, diesen Ruck, diesen Bug,
der den andern nicht glückt.

Auch ich bin dort, wo die Wege nicht gehn,
im Schwaden, den mancher mied,
und ich habe mich oft verlöschen sehn
unter dem Augenlid.

WILL-O'-THE-WISPS

They're old acquaintances of ours,
these lights over the moors.
Like great-aunts they seem to me . . .
More and more clearly I see

the family likeness between us
no circumstance ever smothers:
this curving, swerving, zigzagging impetus
that's beyond the others.

Where no tracks run I too roam about,
in the scud that most have avoided,
and often I've seen myself fizzle out
under my eyelid.

1924

Eine Furche in meinem Hirn,
eine Linie meiner Hand:
hält die Gewohnheit stand,
wird sie mir beides verwirrn.

Rette dich und entflieh
aus dem verengten Netz.
Wirf ein neues Gesetz
über dich und sie.

A furrow in my brain,
a line on my hand:
if habit prevails again
both it will blur, confound.

Save yourself and flee
from the narrowing hem.
Cast a new law
over yourself and them.

September 1924

HANDINNERES

Innres der Hand. Sohle, die nicht mehr geht
als auf Gefühl. Die sich nach oben hält
und im Spiegel
himmlische Straßen empfängt, die selber
wandelnden.
Die gelernt hat, auf Wasser zu gehn,
wenn sie schöpft,
die auf den Brunnen geht,
aller Wege Verwandlerin.
Die auftritt in anderen Händen,
die ihresgleichen
zur Landschaft macht:
wandert und ankommt in ihnen,
sie anfüllt mit Ankunft.

PALM OF THE HAND

Palm of the hand. Sole that has ceased to walk
on anything but feeling. That faces up
and in the mirror
receives heavenly streets, in themselves
mutable.
That has learnt to walk on water
when it fetches water,
that walks over wells,
transmuter of every way.
That appears in other hands,
turning its own kind
into a landscape:
wanders, arrives in them,
with arrival fills them.

October 1924

MAUSOLEUM

Königsherz. Kern eines hohen
Herrscherbaums. Balsamfrucht.
Goldene Herznuß. Urnen-Mohn
mitten im Mittelbau,
(wo der Widerhall abspringt,
wie ein Splitter der Stille,
wenn du dich rührst,
weil es dir scheint,
daß deine vorige
Haltung zu laut war . . .)
Völkern entzogenes,
sterngesinnt,
im unsichtbaren Kreisen
kreisendes Königsherz.

Wo ist, wohin,
jenes der leichten
Lieblingin?
: Lächeln, von außen,
auf die zögernde Rundung
heiterer Früchte gelegt;
oder der Motte, vielleicht,
Kostbarkeit, Florflügel, Fühler . . .

Wo aber, wo, das sie sang,
das sie in Eins sang,
das Dichterherz?
: Wind,
unsichtbar,
Windinnres.

MAUSOLEUM

King's heart. Core of a high
tree of dominion. Balm fruit.
Golden heart-nut. Urn-poppy-seed
in the central tract's centre,
(where the resonance breaks away
like a splinter of stillness
when you stir
because you feel
that your earlier
stance was too noisy . . .)
king's heart
extracted from peoples,
star-minded,
circling in its
invisible orbit.

Where is, gone where,
that of the light
girl, his love?
: smile, laid from outside
on the hesitant roundness
of carefree fruit;
or the moth, perhaps,
preciousness, gauze-wing, feeler . . .

Where, though, what sang her,
what sang her into oneness,
the poet's heart?
: wind,
invisible,
wind's interior.

October 1924

Nacht. Oh du in Tiefe gelöstes
Gesicht an meinem Gesicht.
Du, meines staunenden Anschauns größtes
Übergewicht.

Nacht, in meinem Blicke erschauernd,
aber in sich so fest;
unerschöpfliche Schöpfung, dauernd
über dem Erdenrest;

voll von jungen Gestirnen, die Feuer
aus der Flucht ihres Saums
schleudern ins lautlose Abenteuer
des Zwischenraums:

wie, durch dein bloßes Dasein, erschein ich,
Übertrefferin, klein –;
doch, mit der dunkelen Erde einig,
wag ich es, in dir zu sein.

aus dem Umkreis: Nächte

Night. O face against my face
dissolved into deepness.
You my marvelling look's most immense
preponderance.

Night, in my gaze a spasm,
in yourself made so fast;
inexhaustible genesis, outlasting
earthly remains;

full of young planets that hurl
fire from the flight of their seams
into the soundless adventure
of the space between:

by your mere existence, exceeder,
how small I grow –;
but at one with the darkened earth
I dare be in you.

October 1924, from the unfinished sequence Nights

SCHWERKRAFT

Mitte, wie du aus allen
dich ziehst, auch noch aus Fliegenden dich
wiedergewinnst, Mitte, du Stärkste.

Stehender: wie ein Trank den Durst
durchstürzt ihn die Schwerkraft.

Doch aus dem Schlafenden fällt,
wie aus lagernder Wolke,
reichlicher Regen der Schwere.

GRAVITY

Centre, how from them all
you draw yourself, even from flying creatures
win back yourself, centre, the strongest.

The standing man: as drink through thirst
gravity rushes through him.

But from the sleeper falls,
as from a cloud at rest,
gravity's plentiful rain.

October 1924

Jetzt wär es Zeit, daß Götter träten aus
bewohnten Dingen . . .
Und daß sie jede Wand in meinem Haus
umschlügen. Neue Seite. Nur der Wind,
den solches Blatt im Wenden würfe, reichte hin,
die Luft, wie eine Scholle, umzuschaufeln:
ein neues Atemfeld. Oh Götter, Götter!
Ihr Oftgekommnen, Schläfer in den Dingen,
die heiter aufstehn, die sich an den Brunnen,
die wir vermuten, Hals und Antlitz waschen
und die ihr Ausgeruhtsein leicht hinzutun
zu dem, was voll scheint, unserm vollen Leben.
Noch einmal sei es euer Morgen, Götter.
Wir wiederholen. Ihr allein seid Ursprung.
Die Welt steht auf mit euch, und Anfang glänzt
an allen Bruchstelln unseres Mißlingens . . .

Now it is time that gods came walking out
of things inhabited . . .
And then demolished every wall inside
my house. New page. For nothing but the wind
that would be raised by such a new leaf turning
could turn the air as shovel turns a sod;
a brand-new field of air. O gods, you gods,
the often come who are asleep in things,
cheerfully rise, at wells that we conjecture,
wash wide awake their faces and their necks
and add their restedness to that which seems
full as it is, our lives already full.
Another morning make your morning, gods!
We're the repeaters, only you the source.
Your rising is the world's, beginning shines
from every crack within our patched-up failure . . .

October 1925

Rose, oh reiner Widerspruch, Lust,
Niemandes Schlaf zu sein unter soviel
Lidern.

GONG

Klang, nichtmehr mit Gehör
meßbar. Als wäre der Ton,
der uns rings übertrifft,
eine Reife des Raums.

Rose, pure contradiction, delight
in being nobody's sleep under so many
eyelids.

Epitaph, included in Rilke's last will of October 1925

GONG

Sound by hearing no longer
measurable. As though the tone
that exceeds us all round
were a ripeness of space.

October 1925

IDOL

Gott oder Göttin des Katzenschlafs,
kostende Gottheit, die in dem dunkeln
Mund reife Augen-Beeren zerdrückt,
süßgewordnen Schauns Traubensaft,
ewiges Licht in der Krypta des Gaumens.
Schlaf-Lied nicht, – Gong! Gong!
Was die anderen Götter beschwört,
entläßt diesen verlisteten Gott
an seine einwärts fallende Macht.

IDOL

God or goddess of the sleep of cats,
savouring deity that in the dark
mouth crushes ripe eye-berries,
grape-juice of seeing grown sweet,
everlasting light in the palate's crypt.
Not a lullaby, – gong! gong!
What conjúres other gods
lets him go, this wily god,
to his power that collapses inwards.

November 1925

GONG

Nicht mehr für Ohren . . . : Klang,
der, wie ein tieferes Ohr,
uns, scheinbar Hörende, hört.
Umkehr der Räume. Entwurf
innerer Welten im Frein . . .,
Tempel vor ihrer Geburt,
Lösung, gesättigt mit schwer
löslichen Göttern . . . : Gong!

Summe des Schweigenden, das
sich zu sich selber bekennt,
brausende Einkehr in sich
dessen, das an sich verstummt,
Dauer, aus Ablauf gepreßt,
um-gegossener Stern . . . : Gong!

Du, die man niemals vergißt,
die sich gebar im Verlust,
nichtmehr begriffenes Fest,
Wein an unsichtbarem Mund,
Sturm in der Säule, die trägt,
Wanderers Sturz in den Weg,
unser, an Alles, Verrat . . . : Gong!

GONG

Not meant for ears . . . : boom
that like a deeper ear
hears us, the seemingly hearing.
Reversal of spaces. Draft
of inner worlds outside . . .,
temple before her birth,
dissolution, sated with gods
hard to dissolve . . . : gong!

Sum of what's silent, to
itself only committed,
buzzing return to itself
of that by itself struck silent,
duration squeezed out of motion,
star re-cast . . . : gong!

She whom one never forgets,
who gave birth to herself in loss,
celebration no longer grasped,
wine on invisible lips,
gale in the pillar that bears,
rambler's fall to the path,
our treason, to all . . . : gong!

November 1925

Von nahendem Regen fast zärtlich verdunkelter Garten,
Garten unter der zögernden Hand.
Als besännen sich, ernster, in den Beeten die Arten,
wie es geschah, daß sie ein Gärtner erfand.

Denn sie denken ja ihn; gemischt in die heitere Freiheit
bleibt sein bemühtes Gemüt, bleibt vielleicht sein Verzicht.
Auch an ihnen zerrt, die uns so seltsam erzieht, diese Zweiheit;
noch in dem Leichtesten wecken wir Gegengewicht.

Garden, tenderly darkened, almost, by nearness of rain or
    thunder,
garden under hesitant hands.
As though in their beds more earnestly plants now must wonder
how it could be that a gardener invented their kinds.

For it's of him they are thinking; admixed to pure freedom, their
    trueness,
to them his laborious care, or acceptance of failure, clings.
Even they feel the pull of our curious tutor, that twoness;
we awaken the counterweight in the very lightest of things.

May 1926

ANKUNFT

In einer Rose steht dein Bett, Geliebte. Dich selber
(oh ich Schwimmer wider die Strömung des Dufts)
hab ich verloren. So wie dem Leben zuvor
diese (von außen nicht meßbar) dreimal drei Monate sind,
so, nach innen geschlagen, werd ich erst *sein*. Auf einmal,
zwei Jahrtausende vor jenem neuen Geschöpf,
das wir genießen, wenn die Berührung beginnt,
plötzlich: gegen dir über, werd ich im Auge geboren.

ARRIVAL

Inside a rose your bed stands, beloved. Your very self
(oh, I the swimmer against the current of fragrance)
I have lost. As to my life before now
these (from outside uncountable) three times three months are,
so, beaten inward, not till then shall I *be*. All at once,
two millennia before that new creature
whom we enjoy when the touching begins,
suddenly: faced with you, I am born, in the eye.

early June 1926

Komm du, du letzter, den ich anerkenne,
heilloser Schmerz im leiblichen Geweb:
wie ich im Geiste brannte, sieh, ich brenne
in dir; das Holz hat lange widerstrebt,
der Flamme, die du loderst, zuzustimmen,
nun aber nähr' ich dich und brenn in dir.
Mein hiesig Mildsein wird in deinem Grimmen
ein Grimm der Hölle nicht von hier.
Ganz rein, ganz planlos frei von Zukunft stieg
ich auf des Leidens wirren Scheiterhaufen,
so sicher nirgend Künftiges zu kaufen
um dieses Herz, darin der Vorrat schwieg.
Bin ich es noch, der da unkenntlich brennt?
Erinnerungen reiß ich nicht herein.
O Leben, Leben: Draußensein.
Und ich in Lohe. Niemand der mich kennt.

[Verzicht. Das ist nicht so wie Krankheit war
einst in der Kindheit. Aufschub. Vorwand um
größer zu werden. Alles rief und raunte.
Misch nicht in dieses was dich früh erstaunte]

Now come, the last that I can recognize,
pain, utter pain, fierce in the body's texture.
As once in the mind I burned, so now I burn
in you; the wood resisted, long denied
acceptance to the flame you blazed at me,
but now I feed you and in you I flare.
My mildness here in your hot rage must turn
to hellish rage, hell-fury, kindled there.
Quite pure of forethought, futureless and free
I mounted suffering's tangled, criss-crossed pyre,
so sure there was no purchase to acquire
for this heart's future, all its store now silent.
What burns there, so transmuted, is that I?
Into this fire I drag no memory.
To be alive, alive: to be outside.
And I ablaze. With no one who knows me.

[Renunciation. Not what illness was
in childhood once. Postponement. Pretext for
a growing-up. When all things called, urged on.
That early wonderment, keep it out of this]

December 1926

BLACK SWAN BOOKS
Literary Series

- ☐ H. D., *Hedylus*
- ☐ CARLOS DRUMMOND DE ANDRADE, *The Minus Sign*
- ☐ LAWRENCE DURRELL, *The Ikons*
- ☐ EZRA POUND/JOHN THEOBALD, *Letters*
- ☐ PETER JONES, *The Garden End*
- ☐ *Three Fates in Taos*
- ☐ ADRIAN STOKES, *With All the Views*
- ☐ VERNON WATKINS, *Unity of the Stream*

Catalogue available

Published by
BLACK SWAN BOOKS LTD.
P.O. BOX 327
REDDING RIDGE, CT 06876